The Barnyard Buddies STOP for Peace
Written by Julie D. Penshorn, MBC
Content edited by Rebecca Janke, M.Ed.
Illustrated by Jorry Keith

PCN 2017904914

ISBN 9780998869124

For more information, other books, music, resources for peace, and materials specifically to support the learning about peacemaking in this book, including a recording of the "STOP for Peace" song, other children's music, and a coloring page for children with the STOP for Peace process, please visit: **www.smarttoolsforlife.com**.

Thanks to all our early readers and editors, our families, current events, our conflicts, and Julie's riding students and horses who continually contribute to the making of The Barnyard Buddies.

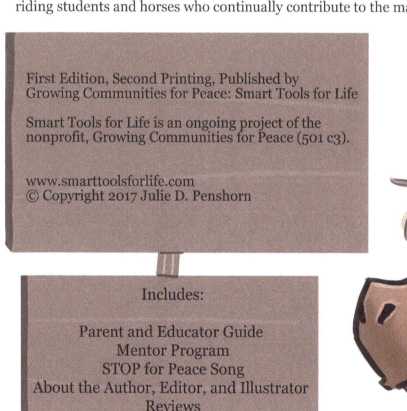

First Edition, Second Printing, Published by Growing Communities for Peace: Smart Tools for Life

Smart Tools for Life is an ongoing project of the nonprofit, Growing Communities for Peace (501 c3).

www.smarttoolsforlife.com
© Copyright 2017 Julie D. Penshorn

Includes:

Parent and Educator Guide
Mentor Program
STOP for Peace Song
About the Author, Editor, and Illustrator
Reviews

Upcoming Titles:

The Barnyard Buddies Dig Up The Truth
The Barnyard Buddies Meet A Refugee

The Barnyard Buddies STOP for Peace

So, they huddled together and stomped to keep warm,
and the rain pelted down. It was quite a storm!
The droplets smacked hard on their hair and their hides,
and it hurt! So they grumbled and their anger did rise.

"I'm mad at King, who stole the best spot,"

said Grey Donkey to Clover, Portland Pig, and Ol' Dot.
The others agreed and their anger grew hot.

Then up spoke a peacemaker, Mrs. McCloud.
She was their good friend, and she was so smart.

She had a good head and a loving heart.

So they breathed

and they blew, as if
cooling their tea.

King made room. He gracefully moved over with courtesy for Ol' Dot, Grey Donkey, Pig, and Clover.

They smiled, and they got warm.
They all could squeeze in.
And they snuggled, and cuddled,
and nestled again.

19

they all said,

About The Creators

Author Julie Penshorn, MBC, makes peace come alive as a way of life for children through engaging, memorable, rhyming literature and music. By using animals with very compelling feelings as the main characters, she bridges her history as a horse trainer and riding teacher with her unique creative talent for making peace education fun!

Content editor, Rebecca Janke, M.Ed., is a peace educator, international columnist, facilitator, community servant and leader, as well as a mentor to university students. She has over 40 years of bringing rich, unique, and practical ideas to families and educators in an entertaining and insightful manner. She specializes in integrating peace into every aspect of the curriculum and promoting peace literacy.

Illustrator, Jorry Keith is a storyboard artist, illustrator, and instructor. She is the writer and the illustrator of the comic book, Seafoam: A Friend for Madison. A strong believer in the arts, and its importance in children's lives, Jorry runs several community-based art classes that guide children through the process of writing and drawing their own comics and books.

Why this book?

The Barnyard Buddies STOP for Peace is a read-aloud book designed to help both children and adults resolve conflicts peacefully. It can contribute to a community-wide culture of peace, especially when combined with a mentor program in pre-schools, classrooms, faith communities and after-school programs. A campaign to encourage community members to self-identify as peacemakers can include this artwork on posters, clothing and more. You'll find information about the **I STOP for Peace** campaign on the **Smart Tools for Life** website.

The **STOP for Peace** process works easily with most other conflict resolution programs. It is memorable and age-appropriate for young children. The **Stop and breathe** step is key. It recognizes that conflict can't be solved until anger and anxiety are toned down to more normal states. Because stopping is so central, we named the whole process with that in mind.

Parent and Educator Guide

After reading the book to the children at least once, the following questions can be explored in the classroom or home. By repeatedly referring to the Barnyard Buddies, Mrs. McCloud, and the story, you can dramatically improve the learning. Playing the music for the children is important for best learning outcomes as well.

1. "Let's learn how to **STOP for Peace** like the Barnyard Buddies! Start by remembering a time when you were angry -- a time you wanted to 'kick or scream or shout'. What can you think of?" Take notes or write on the board. Children feel validated when their thoughts are recorded. Choose a problem to solve and write it on the board or notepaper.

2. "Mrs. McCloud taught the animals that the first step was **S: Stop and breathe**. People can do that too! Breathe in slowly, and then breathe out slowly -- like the animals show us on page nine. When we cool off our hot anger, we breathe like we are cooling off hot tea. We breathe into our bellies, then we blow out slowly. This cools off our angry feelings! Then we don't hurt anyone with our burning hot anger. So, let's do this together. Breathe in slowly: 1, 2, 3. Breathe out slowly: 1, 2, 3. Let's do it a few times. Breathing helps me be more peaceful and then I can think of smart solutions."

3. "When we breathe, we get a better understanding of our feelings. We might not just be angry, we might also be hurt, scared, lonely, frustrated or worried. Let's think about the problem we wrote down and practice expressing our feelings using Mrs. McCloud's second step, **T: Tell how you feel**. We can do that with an *I-Message*.

I-Message example: *I feel frustrated when someone takes all the Legos and I don't have any to work with.* The format is: *I feel* _____ (insert a feeling word) *when someone*_____(insert the problem). Avoid using the word "you". The same negative feelings would arise if someone else used an accusatory word like "you", so avoid provoking defensiveness in your conflict partner.

Visit www.smarttoolsforlife.com/blog for more on this topic, including the "Conflict Resolution Cubes" games and activities to help you work on these skills.

4. "When we know how others feel, it can change how we feel. When our hearts are open, our minds can open and that's the next step from Mrs. McCloud: **O: Open your mind**. What ideas can we think of to solve this problem? When we get lots of ideas we call it *brainstorming*." Record the ideas on the board or notepaper.

5. "The last step to do is **P: Plan a deal**. It's easier after we are cooled off and we know how everyone feels. Sometimes people combine ideas, sometimes they try one, and have a second choice in case their first choice doesn't work. Which idea do you think we should choose first?" Record the idea and the plan so you can keep track of the decision. If it doesn't work well, either try the second choice, if there was one, or simply go back to **O: Open your mind**, and get more ideas.

6. "I am so excited! We've learned how to be peacemakers and **STOP for Peace**! **Congratulations!** To celebrate we can sing the 'Stop for Peace' song!"

7. **Make a journal** so children can continue to draw and write about their peacemaking and conflict resolution experiences all year long. These stories can be shared at www.smarttoolsforlife.com/story anytime, so others can benefit from the children's learning as we build a culture of peace together.

8. **Coloring page and music:** Download a coloring page for the children from the Home page of the website at www.smarttoolsforlife.com. This is a great tool for introducing others to the work you've been doing. This is also the place to find the music, **I STOP for Peace** and **Songs for Peace,** on the Products page. These CDs and downloadable MP3s by Julie Penshorn have music and children's dialogues specifically to support this learning. Either you or your music teacher can teach the children these songs. Music internalizes skills. It's quite common for children to burst forth with songs for peace as they play at home with their families.

Additional Questions and Activities

1. "Who do you think cared about Mrs. McCloud so much that they shared peacemaking skills with her? How did she learn to be a peacemaker? Why was it important?"

2. "How come all but King said they were angry in their I-Messages? Can you imagine some other feelings they may have had? With a different feeling, not anger -- how would that I-message sound for Ol' Dot? Clover? Portland Pig? Grey Donkey?"

3. "What do you think could have helped King be more aware that his buddies were cold?"

4. "If you were to write about, draw, or tell a story about a problem at home or at school, what is that problem? How can it be solved?"

Mentor Program for *The Barnyard Buddies STOP for Peace*

Children ages nine and up can serve as mentors for younger children. Some may need more support from adults. Our experience shows that mentors learn as much, if not more than the younger children. Mentors benefit from an opportunity to serve and know they are needed. That's very powerful. Teens have told us, "I wish someone would have taught this process to me when I was younger. I think I would have had a better life." They also have said, "I felt important! There are some young children who really need to know this!"

Peace literacy: The teachers of younger children are pleased to have a literacy program delivered by older children on this important topic. Enthusiastic older children inspire the younger children to follow suit.

Transportation: Transporting teens to an early childhood or early elementary school may need to follow district guidelines and should be checked. However, elementary school children in the same school with the K-3 grades can easily be mentors.

Training the Mentor Group

Each mentor-trainee needs to become fluent at reading the book out loud, in a clear voice that reaches the back of the classroom. This improves their reading skills and is wonderful training for them as public speakers.

Introduce the book to the mentors by reading it aloud: Read to them as if they were the little children. You will probably like to change your voice for each character's dialogue parts.

Break into pairs and do practice reading and conflict resolution practice: Mentors can have fun with different character voices but remind them to be consistent and clear so the children can understand the message. Mentors then think of a conflict they currently have or have had in the past. Their partner can role-play the conflict partner and they can practice using the **STOP** process together.

Regroup and select all or some mentors to read out-loud: They can learn different ways to deliver the material from each other. Then, invite them to share how they resolved the conflict using the **STOP** process in their practice time.

Role Models: Explain that they now have the opportunity to be long-term role models for the children they visit as they meet up with them in other settings. Ask mentors to share a story about a positive role model or mentor who has impacted them.

Mentor Sessions in the Classroom: Visit One

Mentor introduction by classroom teacher: When the older children visit the classroom, the teacher will gather the young children and introduce the mentor as "Peacemaker _____ (name) who is going to share a very important story of how it's possible to get back to peace when it's been interrupted." Once the mentors are identified this way, they often feel inspired to take this title as part of their identity!

Mentor classroom role: The mentor reads the book as practiced. After reading the story, the mentor can ask about conflicts the children have. The classroom teacher is free to assist the mentor and children. The mentor suggests the children work out their problems using the **STOP for Peace** process and when they are resolved, draw or write a story about how they did it, to share when the mentor returns in a few weeks to a month.

Mentors review the **STOP** process with the children (on page 22) a few times before they leave. Posters of this process are available (please visit the website) that can be displayed in the classroom.

Debriefing Mentors and Preparing for the Second Visit

Meet with the mentors after their first visit. Gather feedback about their experience and how the children responded. Discuss any things they would like new mentors to know, so you can continually improve this process over the years!

Invite mentors to practice with a partner to do a role-play, draw, or write their own conflict story using the **STOP for Peace** process. They will share it next time in the classroom.

Mentor Sessions in the Classroom: Visit Two

Mentors share their STOP for Peace story, listen to and express appreciation for the children's stories, and then collect the artwork. If children have been practicing the music they can sing it for their mentor. Applause is appropriate! **The mentor ends with**, "I'm so proud of all of you. Now, there is a chance for more peace to happen in our school, family, and community because *you* know how to **STOP** for peace."

Mentor follow up: Mentors are responsible for submitting the children's artwork. Convert the children's artwork to individual PDF files and submit with first names of the children to the www.smarttoolsforlife.com website. The young children and their families enjoy seeing the results of this project online and being part of the worldwide STOP for Peace movement. The culture shifts when young people and children take the lead.

It's important that children are validated for developing their newfound skills and recognize that their efforts for peace make a positive impact, worthy of celebration. Welcome the new peacemakers!

STOP for Peace

Julie Penshorn

28

VERSE

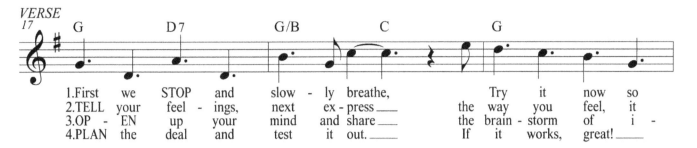

1.First we STOP and slow - ly breathe,   Try it now so
2.TELL your feel - ings, next ex - press____ the way you feel, it
3.OP - EN up your mind and share____ the brain - storm of i -
4.PLAN the deal and test it out.____ If it works, great!____

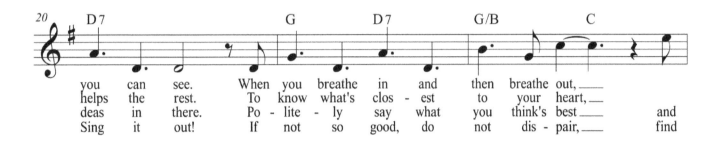

you can see. When you breathe in and then breathe out,____
helps the rest. To know what's clos - est to your heart,____
deas in there. Po - lite - ly say what you think's best____ and
Sing it out! If not so good, do not dis - pair,____ find

You don't need to scream or shout.
ev' - ry - one can tell their part.
lis - ten care - f'ly to the rest.
more i - deas un - der your hair.